Locations - Locations

of

TWD

Seasons 1-6

by

The Location Press

Written by Marlene Littlefield and edited by Jamie Thompson

For information, please contact:

THE LOCATION PRESS
10 Line Creek Rd.
Haralson, GA 30229
First Edition
Printed in the United States of America

ISBN: 978-0-9862992-3-0

Thank You

Locations-Locations of TWD would like to thank our many supporters and contributors. First of all we would like to thank, Jimmy & Marlene Littlefield, Jamie Thompson, Mary Schmidt, Casey Florig and family, Howie Harris, Christina Fernandez, Tammy Vader, Kathy Strickland, Lisa Dupre, Larry Goings, Dustin Baker, Renn Johnson, Sean Watson and especially Bridge to Grace for their music and keeping me sane while I wrote and rewrote this. All of you have been amazing and we're grateful for each and every one of you.

Last but not least we would like to thank Mr. Frank Wilkinson because we wouldn't have any of what we have without him, so we dedicate this book to his memory. He will forever be our firecracker!

Contents

Introduction

In this book, you will be able to find almost every Walking Dead location and some behind the scenes information from seasons 1-6. It is written by fans for the fans who love TWD as much as we do. With the struggles of GPS outages and misinformation, we have compiled this collection of addresses and maps to make your trip easier.

How to use this book:

The locations are numbered by 1, 2, 3 and has a corresponding map to go along with it.

- Every city starts again at one.
- Please remember to be respectful and not trespass.
- Enjoy your personal tour and have fun!

Some locations do not have adresses, that is because at the request of the owner of the property, they do not want anyone there.

PLEASE BE RESPECTFUL TO THE OWNERS WISHES!

From Atlanta to Thomaston, you can find your favorite location in here.

Throughout the book, you will also find information on different tours you can take for certain locations. They have QR Readers where you can scan to find any and all information about the different tours.

If you enjoy TWD as much as we do, we hope that you enjoy this book and find it educational and beneficial.

Atlanta Movie Tours (AMT)

Join Atlanta Movie Tours for a blockbuster adventure taking you to locations of TV shows and movies filmed in Atlanta! From Gone With the Wind to The Walking Dead, Atlanta Movie Tours gives you front row seats for all the action!

Board our luxury coach and sit back as our guides, who have worked on these sets, point out hundreds of locations all over town! Let us show you why Hollywood is closer than you think!

Check us out and book at atlantamovietours.com or call 855-255-FILM (3456) today!

Please respect owners wishes: DO NOT TRESPASS ON ANY PROPERTY!!!

1. Season 1: Episode 1: Hospital: "Days Gone Bye"

Atlanta Mission,
2353 Bolton Rd NW, Atlanta, GA

Rick awakens from his coma when he discovers life is not what it used to be and he is in an abandoned hospital. He confusingly and painfully makes his way outside to find himself surrounded by dead bodies and military vehicles.

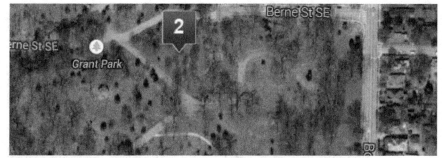

2. Season 1: Episode 1: Park: Bicycle Girl: "Days Gone Bye"
Grant Park, 537 Park Ave SE at Hansell St SE, Atlanta, GA

After leaving Morgan and Dwayne, Rick goes looking for the half bodied walker he had seen before. As he walks through the park, he finds who is now known as "Bicycle Girl" and he approaches her. With tears in his eyes, he raises his gun and says, "I'm sorry this happened to you." and he sadly shoots her in the head.

Bicycle Girl was created with chest pieces, dentures, contacts, along with other outstanding make-up and was shot using a green screen. She wore blue pants to cover the lower half of her body and the rest was CGI to create the entrails, spinal cord, torso pieces and femur bone.

*You can find the back story (webisode) of Bicycle Girl on the TWDSeason One disk or on AMC website.

3. Season 1: Episode 1: Morgan's House: "Days Gone Bye"
376 Ormond St, Atlanta, GA

Rick approaches Morgan's house and Duane attacks him with a shovel thinking he is a walker. Morgan takes Rick in and informs him of what has been happening during his time in the coma.

4. Season 1: Episode 1: Rick's House: "Days Gone Bye"

817 Cherokee Ave SE, Atlanta, GA

Rick returns to his home to see if he can find his family only to find an empty house. He searches for pictures and any hope that his family is still alive.

5. Season 1: Episode 1: The Sheriff's Office "Days Gone Bye"

Vesta Holdings, 1737 Ellsworth Industrial Blvd NW, Atlanta, GA

Rick, Morgan and Duane head out looking for weapons and vehicles. They enter the "Sheriff's Office" where they are able to take a hot shower. As they are leaving, Rick hands Morgan a radio and tells him he will turn his radio on every day at dawn and he should do the same too.

*The inside of the Sheriff's office was recreated in Season 3 Episode 12 "Clear" at 16 Main St, in Grantville, GA.

6. Season 1: Episode 1: The Bridge and Entrance: "Days Gone Bye"

Parkway Dr. NE, Atlanta, GA (Off Jimmy Carter Pkwy)

Rick approaches Atlanta on horseback overlooking Freedom Parkway in this memorable and historic scene that has been used on posters and season one DVD and Blu-ray covers.

*Actual shots from this scene were shot on the bridge off Nelson St, Spring St SW and were graphically enhanced to make it look like it was taken in one shot.

7. Season 1: Episodes 1 and 2: The Tank: "Days Gone Bye" and "Guts"

Forsyth-Walton Building, 52 Walton St NW and Forsyth St, Atlanta, GA

Rick is stuck in the tank, with the help of Glenn, they escape into the alley.
The final shot from this episode was taken from the front side of this building. Rick is barricaded inside the tank with hundreds of walkers surrounding him. The final shot shows a top view of the tank with walkers on every side. The shot was in likeness to the comics.

8. Season 1: Episode 2 and 3: Merle's Hand (The Roof) and The Truck: "Guts" and "Tell It to the Frogs"

Norfolk Southern Building, 95 Spring Street SW and Mitchell St SW, Atlanta, GA

•S1E2 "Guts"

The department store where Rick first meets the survivors, later he handcuffs Merle to the top of the building and Merle cuts off his hand. During filming on the rooftop of the Norfolk Southern Building, Due to the gunfire, people were scattering on the streets below and the actual swat team was called out. It was quickly resolved when they were notified that they were shooting a television show.

•S1E3 "Tell It to the Frogs"

Glenn, Rick, T-Dog and Daryl return to Atlanta to look for Merle. They park the truck and return later to find the truck has been stolen.

9. Season 1: Episode 2: Blending In: "Guts"
Lunacy Black Market, 231 Mitchell St SW, Atlanta, GA

Rick and Glenn cover themselves with walker guts to blend in with the horde of impeding walkers. As they walk in the streets, the walkers seem to pass right by them until it begins to rain.

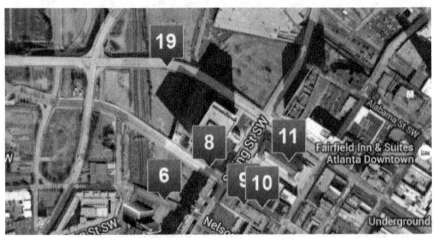

10. Season 1: Episode 2: The Escape: "Guts"
The Exchange, 222 Mitchell St SW Forsyth St. SW, Atlanta, GA

Rick and Glenn have escaped the walkers by climbing up a ladder; they enter the top of this building where they enter into the "Department Store." They rescue the others in the box truck.

Box truck route

When Rick returns back to Atlanta to look for Merle in S1E3 "Tell It to the Frogs" He parks the box truck in the rail yard on Spring St SW and Nelson Ave.

11. Season 1: Episode 2: The Charger: "Guts"

Martin Luther King Jr Federal Building, 77 Forsyth St SW, Atlanta, GA

Glenn steals a Dodge Charger to draw away the walkers and proceeds to drive to camp with the alarm system blaring so Rick can escape with the other survivors.

12. Season 1: Episodes 2-5: The Quarry and Camp

Westside Park—Bellwood Quarry, Chappell Rd NW, Atlanta, GA

Episodes of the Quarry and Camp:

- •S1E2 "Guts"
- •S1E3 "Tell It to the Frogs"
- •S1E4 "Vatos"
- •S1E5 "Wildfire"

At the groups of survivor camp, Shane teaches Carl how to hunt for frogs, Andrea and Amy fish and the ladies wash clothes. Shane becomes outraged as he sees Ed hit Carol and beats Ed beyond recognition. Carol becomes distraught as she sees Ed beaten and begs him for forgiveness.

Atlanta BeltLine Tours offers tours of The Quarry

13. Season 1: Episode 4: Abandoned Building: "Vatos"

The Goat Farm/Murray's Mill,
1200 Foster St at Huff Rd, Atlanta, GA

Glenn is taken hostage by a gang of men. Rick and the group then take one of their men hostage and they learn of their hideout. After talking with the men, they find out the "Vatos" are really hiding that they are just a group taking care of sick and elderly people.

14. Season 1: Episode 4: The Retirement Home: "Vatos"

20 WM Holmes Borders Dr NE, Atlanta, GA

Rick, Daryl and T-Dog follow the "Vatos" into this building where elderly and sick people have taken refuge.

15. Season 1: Episodes 5-6: CDC: "Wildfire" and "TS-19"

Cobb Energy Performing Arts Centre
2800 Cobb Galleria Pkwy, Atlanta, GA

The group arrives at the CDC in hopes for answers to find Scientist Edwin Jenner has barricaded himself in the building. After hot showers and a relaxing evening of fun, Jenner shows them test subject "TS-19". Later on, Rick discovers that they are, "ALL INFECTED" and when the power supply runs out, the building destroys itself and the group escapes, losing a member along the way because of her own choice.

16. Season 4: Episode 4: Veterinary School: "Indifference"

Morris Brown College, 643 Martin Luther King Jr Dr. SW, Atlanta, GA

Daryl, Michonne, Tyreese and Bob make it to the veterinary hospital and find the medicine. Bob's bag is grabbed by walkers and Daryl is outraged to find that it contains alcohol. Daryl tells Bob he will beat him beyond recognition if he drinks any before the sick people get their medication.

17. Season 4 and 5: TERMINUS

Collier Metals, 95 Windsor Street SW, Atlanta, GA

•S4E15 "Us"

Maggie, Glenn, Sasha, Bob, Abraham, Rosita and Eugene reach the base of Terminus. As they enter, they see the sign "TERMINUS" on the outside of the building. They cautiously enter the premises where Mary is waiting to greet them. They do not know they're cannibals.

•S4E16 "A"

Daryl, Rick, Michonne and Carl find Terminus, they are cautious as they enter burying their guns on the way. When they enter, they find a woman trying to reach out on the radio to people to bring them to Terminus and another group that has them put down their weapon. They are taken through the complex only to find that the survivors there are wearing the clothes of their friends they have been separated from. A fight ensues and they are ordered to enter a box car with the letter "A" clearly written on the side of it. Inside is where they find most of the remaining members of their group.

* Scenes from the train car in season four were filmed in Senoia on the railroad tracks near Senoia Coffee House and Café.

•S5E1 "No Sanctuary"

Rick, Daryl, Glenn and Bob are taken hostage and almost killed by the Termites before breaking free. Carol blows up tank to deter walkers so the group can escape.

18. Season 5: Episode 6: Carol Gets Hit By Car: "Consumed"
50 Hurt Plaza NE, Atlanta, GA

Carol is trying to escape the building and gets hit with a car by Grady cops. They take her back to Grady to heal her from her injuries.

19. Season : Episode 6: Van Falls Off Bridge: "Consumed"
MLK JR Dr. NW (Near Spring St.), Atlanta, GA

Carol and Daryl try to escape walkers and jump into a van that is hanging off a bridge. The van falls to the ground below injuring Carol.

20. Season 5" Episode 6: Noah Steal's Daryl's Crossbow: "Consumed"

Carnegie Way NW (Near Westin Hotel, downtown), Atlanta, GA

Daryl and Carol run into Noah the he tries to steal their weapons and leave them to die.

21. Season 5: Episode 8: Rick Confronts Hospital Cops: "CODA"

(Parking Deck) 150 Carnegie Way NW, Atlanta, GA

Rick confronts the hospital cops as he tries to convince them to make a deal to get Carol and Beth back from Grady Memorial Hospital.

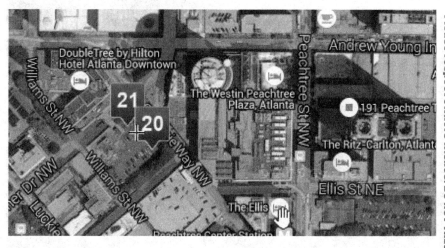

Douglasville

1. Season 1: Episode 5: The Group Leaves Jim: "Wildfire"

Riverside Pkwy near Lower River Rd, Douglasville, GA

Jim was bitten by a walker at the camp and had become very ill. He asks the group to leave him behind so he can "be with his family."

Many people believed that the zombie on the Season 4 DVD boxed set was referenced to Jim. It in fact was not but the writers of "The Walking Dead" like to throw in many similarities and "Easter Eggs" for us to catch on to.

Mansfield

1. Season 1: Episode 1: Rick & Shane Have Lunch: "Days Gone Bye"
3092 GA-11 N, Mansfield, GA

Shane and Rick are eating lunch when alerted to an emergency call on the radio. They quickly drive off.

2. Season 1: Episode 1: Car Crash Scene: "Days Gone Bye"
Spears Lane, Mansfield, GA

Rick and Shane and others from the police force set up a road block with spikes to stop a car, the car flips and men emerge from the car and one shoots Rick.

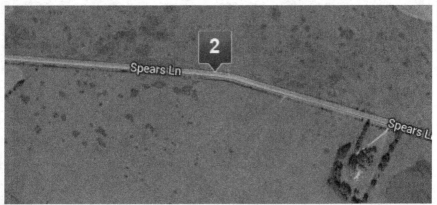

3. Season 1: Episode 1: Rick Finds Horse: "Days Gone Bye"
24399 Maddox St, Mansfield, GA

Rick runs out of gas in his patrol car and goes searching for transportation. He runs into this old farmhouse where he looks through the window to find people who have committed suicide and the words, "God Forgive Us" written over them. He searches around the home only to find a horse in the pasture that he later rides into Atlanta.

1. Season 1: Opening Scene: "Days Gone Bye"

Texaco Station, 3939 Cascade Palmetto Hwy, Fairburn, GA

Rick approached the gas station with gas can in hand. He walks down the hill between the sign only to find a little girl walking by herself in her pajamas with teddy bear in tow. He calls out to the little girl and as she turns, she charges Rick, and he lifts his gun and reluctantly shoots her in the head.

Please respect owners wishes: DO NOT TRESPASS ON ANY PROPERTY!!!

Palmetto

1. Season 2: Episode 5: Daryl's Search: "Chupacabra"

Cochran Mill Nature Center, 6300 Cochran Mill Rd, Palmetto, GA

Daryl borrows a horse and finds Sophia's doll in a creek. The horse throws him and runs away after coming across a snake on the path. Daryl is thrown down a steep hillside and one of his crossbow arrows stabs him in the side. Daryl then has a vision of his missing brother Merle, where he heckles him, saying that the other survivors do not respect Daryl. Merle harasses him for spending more time searching for Sophia than for his brother. After he awakens, he kills a walker that is trying to eat his shoe; he then makes a necklace out of their ears before once more attempting to climb the hill. Exhausted and tired of the taunts of his brother in his visions, he makes it to the top and makes his way back to the farm.

* There is at least a half mile hike to this location.

Peachtree City

1. Season 2: Episode 2: Bad News: "Bloodletting"
Peachtree City Elementary School, 201 Wisdom Rd, Peachtree City GA

In a flashback, Shane pulls up to the school where Lori is standing and speaking to some other women. He tells Lori that Rick has been badly injured in a shootout and Lori then tells Carl.

This is a functioning school, DO NOT ENTER when children are present.

2. Season 4: Episode 7: Walker Pete: "Dead Weight"
Glenloch Recreation Center, 601 Stevens Entry, Peachtree City, GA

Stunt scenes of Walker Pete were filmed in this location.

*The original location is filmed at Raleigh Studios in Senoia, GA.

3. Season 5: Episode 9: The Group Comes Out of the Woods: "What's Happening and What's Going On"

Shirewilt Estates, Redwine Rd, Peachtree City, GA

Rick and the group are looking for a safe place to stay and approach Noah's home. When they get to the gate, they find that it had been attacked and that there are possibly no survivors.

4. Season 5: Episode 9: Noah's Cries: "What's Happening and What's Going On"

Shirewilt Estates, Summer Place and Kraftwood Park, Peachtree City, GA

Noah sees what had become of his old neighborhood and falls to the ground and cries.

5. Season 5: Episode 9: Noah's House: "What's Happening and What's Going On"

Shirewilt Estates, 343 Summer Place, Peachtree City, GA

Noah runs to see what has become of his family and Tyreese runs after him. When they enter the house, they find that Noah's mother had died so

Noah covers her with a rug. Tyreese explores the house then, while he was in Noah's brother's room, he was bitten on the arm.

Due to blood loss, Tyreese had visions of Martin, The Governor, Beth, Lizzy and Mika. Sadly, after the group attempts to save him, Tyresse dies.

*Scenes from the bedroom were recreated at Raleigh Studios due to the blood loss that Tyreese was going to experience.

6. Season 5: Episode 9: Michonne's Discussion: "What's Happening and What's Going On"

Shirewilt Estates, 105 Kraftwood Park, Peachtree City, GA

Michonne and Rick pick up some supplies and have a discussion with Glenn. During their search they find a baseball jersey and a bat.

Newnan

Newnan is known as a The City of Homes. During the Civil War, most of Georgia was burned, yet Newnan was spared because it was the home to General Sherman's aunt and also a Union Hospital. Throughout the years, Newnan has also been home to many movies. Zombieland with Woody Harrelson, Fried Green Tomatoes and Driving Miss Daisy staring Jessica Tandy and Murder in Coweta County starring Andy Griffith and Johnny Cash.

More recent movies include, The Killers starring Katherine Heigl and Aston Kutcher, A Time to Kill starring Matthew McConaughey and Sandra Bullock, Sweet Home Alabama with Reese Witherspoon and don't forget The Walking Dead.

1. Season 2: Episodes 2 and 3: FEMA Camp: "Bloodletting" and "Save the Last One"

Newnan High School, 190 Lagrange St, Newnan, GA

Shane and Otis go on a run to search for medical supplies for Carl at a nearby FEMA Camp. After getting the supplies, Shane shoots Otis in the leg leaving him for the walkers to eat so he can escape.

*This is a public school. DO NOT ENTER the property when school is in session or children are present.

2. Season 3: Episode 5: Daycare: "Say the Word"

Son Rise Baptist Church, 6 Shenandoah Blvd, Newnan, GA

Daryl and Maggie go searching for formula for baby Judith. While inside, Daryl kills a possum for the group to eat later.

3. Season 3: The Arena
Caldwell Tanks, 57 E Broad St, Newnan, GA

Episodes of "The Arena":

•S3E5: "Say the Word"
•S3E8: "Made to Suffer"
•S3E9: "The Suicide King"

Merle and Martinez fight to amuse Woodbury resident with chained up walkers in the background. Andrea is there to witness it and gets angry with the Governor.

Michonne finds walkers in a cage and proceeds to kill them all; Shumpert comes and finds what she has done.

*This building has also been used in the filming of Hunger Games Mocking Jay.

4. Season 5: Episode 11: Aaron and Eric Reunited: "The Distance"

Caldwell Tanks, 57 E Broad St, Newnan, GA

The group is back together and Rick tells Aaron that he can't stay with Eric who had broken his ankle. Aaron is determined to stay with his boyfriend.

5. Season 3: Episode 15: Merle Uses Michonne's Sword: "This Sorrowful Life"

Pintail Dr, Newnan, GA

Merle uses Michonne's sword to kill walkers on his way back to Woodbury after kidnapping Michonne.

6. Season 3: Episode 15: Broken down Car: "This Sorrowful Life"

150 Pintail Dr, Newnan, GA

After Merle kidnaps Michonne, they go looking for a vehicle, when he finds the vehicle doesn't work, they move on.

7. Season 3: Episode 15: Merle ties up Michonne: "This Sorrowful Life"
Oaks Inn, 1057 Highway 29 S, Newnan, GA

Merle has Michonne tied up; he is hotwiring the car when walkers start attacking. Michonne kills the walkers and they make their escape.

*The room that was used for the walker scene was room 8. Michonne was tied up outside the door and the black mark from where she filmed is still clear on the pole to this day. As seen in the picture.

8. Season 4: Episode 3: Medicine Run: "Isolation"
Plant Yates, 708 Dyer Road Highway Alt 27 Newnan, GA

Daryl, Bob, Michonne and Tyreese go on a supply run for antibiotics to keep the sickness going throughout the prison. While on the road, they become surrounded by hundreds of walkers.

*Driving scenes from this episode were filmed on Dolly Nixon Rd in Senoia, GA.

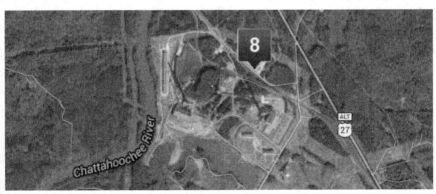

9. Season 4: Episode 6: Nursing Home: "Live Bait"

Old Papp Clinic, 15 Cavendar St., Newnan, GA

Lilly sends the Governor a.k.a. "Brian Heriot" on a run to get oxygen for her dying father.

10. Season 4: Episode 6: The Burial Site: "Live Bait"

Empty Lot on Charmichael St, Newnan, GA
(Behind the old Newnan Hospital and the new West Georgia Tech)

Lilly and the Governor bury Lilly's dad.

*During filming, scenes were shot of Lilly walking through the fence to kill a walker. Scenes were cut and never shown in the deleted scenes.

11. Season 4: Episode 11: Search for Maggie: "Claimed"

Goodwyn Rd. Newnan, GA

Glenn, Abraham, Eugene, Rosita and Tara go searching for Maggie. They walk down this road.

12. Season 4: Episode 11: Clearing the Road: "Claimed"
E Murphy St, Newnan, GA

Abraham stops the truck to clear the road of walkers. As Tara attempts to shoot the walkers, Abraham kills them with a crowbar. Tara wonders why Abraham smiles as he kills them and he replies that he is the "luckiest guy in the world."

13. Season 4: Episode 13: Bob, Sasha and Maggie find Terminus Sign: "Alone"
Bill Hart Rd near Joe Cox Rd, Newnan, GA

Bob, Sasha and Maggie come across some tracks where they see a sign inviting them to Terminus. Bob tells the ladies about the radio broadcast he heard in the car with Tyreese, Daryl and Michonne in S4E3. Maggie insists they go there, hoping to find Glenn.

14. Season 4: Episode 13: Maggie Leaves a Message: "Alone"
E Newnan Rd, Newnan, GA

Maggie follows the tracks in search for Terminus. She comes across a walker that she kills in order to leave a note for Glenn in blood at the RR crossing.

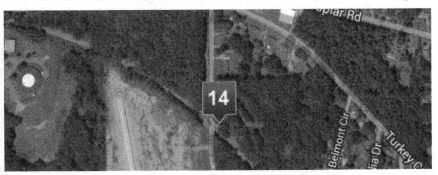

15. Season 4: Episode 13: Another Message: "Alone"

Murphy St, Newnan, GA

Bob and Sasha come across another message from Maggie for Glenn.

16. Season 4: Episode 13: Bob and Sasha Kiss: "Alone"

First St RR Tracks, Newnan, GA
(Next to Bridging the Gap: SEE BELOW)

Bob confides in Sasha and kisses her. Sasha breaks away from Bob to go find Maggie.

17. Season 4: Episode 13: Sasha finds Maggie: "Alone"

Bridging the Gap, 19 1st Avenue, Newnan, GA

Sasha is taking some time alone to try to come to grips with what has happened. She looks out the window of the 3 story building and sees Maggie lying amongst the walkers.

18. Season 4: Episode 13: Marauders Find Daryl: "Alone"

Joe Cox Rd and Bill Hart Rd RR Crossing, Newnan, GA

Daryl collapses in the road then cried while searching for Beth. The Marauders walk up on him and take him into their group.

19. Season 4: Episode 15: Abraham's Army Finds a Minivan: "Us"

Raymond Ray St, Newnan, GA

Abraham, Rosita and Eugene find a minivan with the words "let momma be" on it. They kill the walker inside and drive off.

20. Season 4: Episode 15: The Walker Tower: "Us"

Goodwyn Rd, Newnan, GA

Abraham, Eugene, Rosita, Tara and Glenn come across a tower where a walker falls from the top of it. The walker almost falls on Eugene whom Abraham saves causing Tara to fall and hurt her leg. Abraham wants to rest but Glenn decides to go on. Abraham gives Glenn the riot gear that he has to protect Eugene.

21. Season 5: Grady Memorial Hospital

Old Newnan Piedmont Hospital, 60 Hospital Road Newnan, GA

Episodes of Grady Memorial Hospital:

- **S5E4: "Slabtown"**
- **S5E7: "Crossed"**
- **S5E8: "Coda"**

After Beth's disappearance, she resurfaces at Grady Memorial Hospital which was actually filmed at the Old Newnan Piedmont Hospital. Green screens were used to show the areas of Atlanta in the background.

*This is where Noah was introduced and where Beth sadly met her demise.

22. Season 5: Episode 10: The Group Finds Friendly Water: "Them"

E Gordon Rd, Newnan, GA (Just past East Newnan Baptist Church)

The group finds water in the road from a "friend". It begins to rain and Daryl informs them of a barn. He walks through

the woods to the barn.

*Barn is located in Williamson

23. Season 6: Episode 1: Quarry: "First Time Again"
Vulcan Mineral Comany, 256 Elzie Johnson Rd, Newnan, GA

Rick and Morga discover a quarry that has been keeping walkers out of Alexandria. Rick figures out a way to lure the walkers away.

Grantville

Grantville has been the home of 5 different movie productions and 3 episodes of "The Walking Dead"." The War" with Kevin Costner was filmed there in 1994. "Broken Bridges" followed with Kelly Preston, Toby Keith and Burt Reynolds in 2006, "Lawless" with Shia LeBeouf in 2012. Then Jim Carrey and Jeff Daniels came to town to film "Dumb and Dumber To" in 2013 followed by Vince Vaughn in 2014 for "Term Life".

With all the movie productions going on in this small town, you would think the fans would be flocking the town. Such is not the case until The Walking Dead came to town. With the recreation of Morgan's Apartment, fans from all over the world have come to see the amazing transformation that takes them back to the days of Morgan Jones.

Morgan's Apartment has been recreated by Jonathan Toste and Patrick Paramore, Jr. into what you saw on the episode.

Grantville Dead Walking Tour

1. Season 3: Episode 12: Morgan's Apartment: "Clear"
16 Main St (upstairs), Grantville, GA

Rick, Michonne and Carl are on a supply run. They return to Rick and Carl's home of King County to find the walls of the town graffitied with sayings such as "Away With You" on the wall and "Turn Around and Live" in the crosswalk. All of downtown Grantville was used for the filming. Barricades and booby traps were used in the scenes of this episode.

2. Season 3: Episode 12: The Sheriff's Office: "Clear"
16 Main St., Grantville, GA

Rick returns to his old Sheriff's Office to retrieve some guns only to find the guns have all been removed.

As they walk toward town, they find a madman shooting at them from the roof. They take refuge behind vehicles as the shooting occurs, when the madman comes down from the roof, Carl shoots him. Then they travel up booby trapped stairs to find Morgan's domicile. Inside the apartment, they find the walls graffitied with chalk and spray paint with nonsense sayings and the words "clear" all over them.

3. Season 3: Episode 12: The Baby Store: "Clear"
5 LaGrange St, Grantville, GA 30220

Carl decides he would like to get a crib for his baby sister. After much debate, Michonne goes walking with him as Carl ducks around the corner from her, she swiftly runs after him and they approach "The Baby Store".

4. Season 3: Episode 12: Kings County Café: "Clear"
Old Train Depot, Main St, Grantville, GA

After retrieving the crib, Carl decides he would like to get just one more thing for baby Judith. Michonne and Carl head straight and end up at Kings County Café. As Michonne and Carl detour the walkers inside the café, they approach the bar area where they retrieve a small picture of the Grimes family. The walker bartender awakes from his slumber to try to attack the pair and they make a swift exit only to find that Carl has dropped his picture. Michonne takes off to the right appearing to go around the back of the café, returning with picture and Paper Mache cat in tow.

5. Season 3: Episode 12: The Wall: "Clear" and Opening Credits
Church St, Grantville, GA

As Rick, Michonne and Carl enter the town; they pass a wall that states, "Away With You" on it. As they leave the town; they pass the same wall and Morgan is behind the wall burning the walker bodies.

6. Season 3: Episode 13: The Governor Chases Andrea: "Prey"
Old Grantville Mill, Grady St. Grantville, GA

Andrea is trying to flee from the Governor; she runs through the woods and comes out by this building. As she enters the building she runs into more than she bargains for.

7/8. Season 4: Episode 13: The Funeral Home and Cemetery: "Alone" Funeral Home
26 Magnolia Ln, Grantville, GA

Daryl and Beth take refuge in the funeral home. They fill their bellies with a "Redneck Brunch" as Beth sings and Daryl rests in the coffin. They are later met by a one-eyed dog and separated when Daryl is left to kill walkers. Beth is later kidnapped leaving Daryl alone.

*Scenes from the basement were filmed at Raleigh Studio's in Senoia, GA

Cemetery
Griffin St, Grantville, GA

Daryl and Beth walk through the cemetery to reach the funeral home. Scenes in the cemetery were filmed in front of a large green screen to show that the funeral home sat on cemetery property.

*All driving scenes from "Clear" were filmed in Hogansville, GA on Coweta Heard Rd.

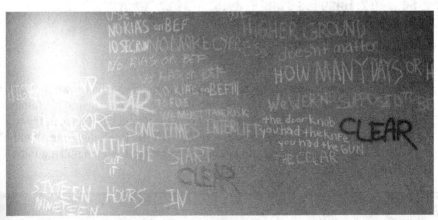

Sharpsburg

1. Season 2: Episodes 4 and 6: Steve's Pharmacy: "Cherokee Rose" and "Secrets"

96 Main Street, Sharpsburg GA

•S2E4 "Cherokee Rose"

Lori asks Glenn to get her a secret product on his supply run. Glenn is surprised at what he sees on her list. When Maggie asks what Glenn is looking for, he says a box of condoms and Maggie then proceeds to seduce Glenn.

•S2E5 "Secrets"

Glenn and Maggie are sent back to the pharmacy to get the morning after pill for Lori.

2. Season 2: Episodes 8 and 9: Hershel's Bar: "Nebraska" and "Triggerfinger"

132 Terrentine Rd, Sharpsburg, GA

•S2E8 "Nebraska"

Rick and Glenn find Hershel in the town bar, where he has reverted back to his old alcoholic ways. Rick persuades Hershel to return to his family, just as two survivors (Dave and Tony) come into the bar. The men try to get out of Rick, the location of the farm. After Rick refuses to let them know about the whereabouts of their safe haven, the men pull a gun on Rick, and then Rick shoots them.

•S2E9 "Triggerfinger"

After killing the two men, Rick, Hershel, and Glenn try to leave; three other men arrive in town looking for Dave and Tony. Rick, Hershel, and Glenn remain in the bar. A fight breaks out after Rick tells the men that he killed their friend's in self-defense.

*Between Steve's Pharmacy and The Old Carriage House, is the alley where one of the men got his leg stuck on the steel fence. The fence was a prop and does not really exist.

3. Season 2: Episode 9: Leg Stuck on Fence: "Triggerfinger"

Main St (Between Steve's Pharmacy and Carriage House)

Rick, Hershel and Glenn are trying to escape the bar. A man is shooting at them when a truck pulls up and the man inside tells him to jump. When he jumps his leg gets caught on the iron fence. Hershel attempts to cut off his leg when walkers approach and is unsuccessful so Rick rips his leg off the fence.

Moreland

1. Opening Credits: The Cemetery

Gordon Road Church of Christ, 1211 Gordon Rd, Moreland, GA

Cemetery is featured in every opening credit in seasons 2-4.

2. Season 5: Episode 10: Sasha Goes Crazy on Bridge: "Them"

Gordon Rd, Moreland, GA (closest address is 1696 Gordon Rd.)

The group is suffering from fatigue from walking when they come across a hoard of walkers on the bridge. Rick kills the walkers and throws them down the canal when Sasha starts going crazy and starts killing walkers like mad and cuts Abraham's arm in the process.

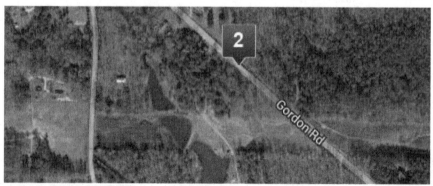

Please respect owners wishes: DO NOT TRESPASS ON ANY PROPERTY!!!

Turin

1. Season 3: Episode 1: Old House: "Seed"
565 Reese Rd, Turin, GA

The group searches for a safe place to stay and food. They vacate the house of walkers and Carl searches the cabinets for food and finds dog food. As he tries to open the cans, Rick hurls them into the fireplace. T-Dog notices a horde of walkers heading toward the house so the group makes a run for it.

2. Season 3: Episode 5 and 14: Season 4: Episode 8: The Walker Pits: "Say the Word, Prey and Dead Weight"
81 Hunter St, Turin, GA

•S3E5 "Say the Word"
Michonne has decapitated all of the captive walkers at the arena; the Governor sends Merle and Milton to retrieve more.

•S3E14 "Prey"

Tyreese and Sasha find out what the walkers are being used for in the walker pit. Tyreese and Allen get into a fight.

•S4E7 "Dead Weight"

The Governor and Martinez are hitting golf balls off the camper; the Governor hits Martinez upside the head and drags him to the pits and feeds him to the walkers.

*The walker pits were filmed here. The campsite was filmed at Raleigh Studios.

N Hunter and Odom Rd

3. Season 4: Episode 6: Fleeing Walkers: "Live Bait"

N Hunter St and Odom Rd, Turin, GA

The Governor, Lilly, Tara and Meaghan flee walkers after setting off on foot when their truck won't start.

4. Season 4: Episode 10: The Prison Bus: "Inmates"

Reese Rd, Turin, GA

Maggie, Sasha and Bob come across the prison bus and search it in hopes of finding Glenn.

5. Season 4: Episode 12: The Moonshine House: "Still"

McIntosh Trail, Turin, GA

Daryl takes Beth to a rundown house that he said he had found earlier with Michonne. He pours her some moonshine and she asks him to play a drinking game with her where Daryl becomes intoxicated. Daryl tries to force Beth to use his crossbow and kill a walker and Beth refuses. They argue about different events and Daryl begins to cry about things brought up from his past and Beth consoles him.

They are discussing Daryl's tortured past and Daryl tells Beth they need more to drink. They then pour out all the moonshine all over the house and flip the house off as they watch it burn to the ground.

*The production company was given permission by the owner to burn the house, due to the fact it was about to be bulldozed.

6. Season 5: Episode 9: Drive-By Cabin: "What Happened and What's Going On"

Reece Rd, Turin, GA (Next to "Seed" House)

The group is looking for Noah's house and passes by this cabin. Rick is talking to Carol on the walkie-talkie.

Senoia

Senoia is a small town with a huge history not only in a historical aspect. A film history that dates back to the late 70's and early 80's with Guyana Tragedy the Story of Jim Jones, Pet Sematary Two, Driving Miss Daisy and Fried Green Tomatoes. To present day, a total of approximately 22 movies have been filmed in the area and since 2009 The Walking Dead has called Senoia home.

As you stroll through the streets, you can recall Andrea's speech to the town or even the Governors famous, "Welcome to Woodbury" as he exited "Woodbury Town Hall". Senoia is also the host of the Southern Living Home which has also been used in scenes from TWD.

The official Woodbury Shoppe is located at 48 Main St. This a one stop shop for all your AMC Walking Dead Merchandise. While you shop, visit the museum downstairs. You never know who you will meet inside the shop. Please note that some locations are repeated for different episodes in Senoia.

1. Season 2: Episode 1: Sophia's Church: "What Lies Ahead"

2325 Luther Bailey Rd., Senoia, GA

The group goes searching for Sophia, as they run through the graveyard, Daryl enters the church asking, "JC if he is taking any requests."

Season 2: Hershel's Farm

Senoia, GA

Hershel's farm is a very iconic part of The Walking Dead history BUT, this is a private family home! At the request of the owners, we are not giving out any information on the location of this property other than what was filmed there. Just remember the farm looks exactly the same as it looked like on the show.

PLEASE RESPECT THE OWNERS PRIVACY! IF YOU TRESPASS YOU WILL GO TO JAIL!!!

Episodes of "Hershel's Farm":

- **S2E2: "Bloodletting"**
- **S2E3: "Save the Last One"**
- **S2E4: "Cherokee Rose"**
- **S2E5: "Chupacabra"**
- **S2E6: "Secrets"**
- **S2E7: "Pretty Much Dead Already"**
- **S2E8: "Nebraska"**
- **S2E9: "Triggerfinger"**
- **S2E10: "18 Miles Out"**
- **S2E11: "Judge, Jury, Executioner"**
- **S2E12: "Better Angels"**
- **S2E13: "Beside the Dying Fire"**

This property is where the group took refuge in most of Season 2. Many scenes were filmed here including the barn scenes. This property is private property and owners are adamant about not having people on their property.

DO NOT ENTER

*During the walker massacre at the barn, several guns were used including, three nine millimeters and two shotguns.

**As Sophia exited the barn, her walker attire had been softened to make you ask the question, "Is she really dead?" There was a total of eight episodes spent looking for Sophia.

***Wonder how they burned the walkers? A stuntman was put in front of a black screen with two layers of specially flame retarded soaked clothing, a rain coat and more clothing. The stuntman was allowed to burn for 7-8 seconds and then put out by a fire extinguisher. The shot was used to enhance the walkers on fire in the barn.

2. Season 2: Episode 6: Shane and Andrea Search for Sophia: "Secrets"

Hutchinson Cove, Emerald Way, Senoia, GA

Andrea and Shane go looking for Sophia; Shane is teaching Andrea how to better her shooting skills when walkers try to take them over. When they return to the car, Andrea seduces Shane.

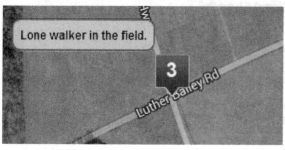

Lone walker in the field.

3. Season 2: Episode 10: Rick and Shane Conversation: "18 Miles Out"

Cocks Crossroads, Cross section of Old Hwy 85 and Luther Bailey, Senoia, GA

Rick and Shane are looking for a location to drop off Randall whom they have taken captive. Rick has a serious conversation with Shane about Lori. Lone walker moves through the field.

4. Season 2: Episode 13: Walkers Come Through the Fence: "Besides the Dying Fire"

Rockhorse Riding Center, 1000 Rockhouse Road, Senoia, GA

Walkers are approaching the farm. A horde gets to a fence and breaks through the fence. Walkers are walking through the woods and hear the gunshot from Carl shooting Shane and change course and go toward the farm.

5. Season 2: Episode 13: The Campsite: "Beside the Dying Fire"
Elder's Mill Waterfall and Campsite, 1739 Elder's Mill Rd, Senoia, GA

Rick runs out of gas in the Suburban. The group tries to pull together a plan of action to stay safe for the night. Rick reveals to the group that "they're all infected." The group takes refuge in the camp as the prison lingers in the background. Rick declares his "Ricktatorship" as the group hopes for a brighter future and safety.

Elders Mill Waterfall and Campsite

6. Seasons 3-4: The Prison/Raliegh Studios
Season 4: Episode 7: The Dock: "Dead Weight"
Season 5: Episode 1: Cannibal's Cabin: "No Sanctuary"
Season 5: Father Gabriel's Church
Season 5: Episode 14: Alexandria Construction: "Spend"
Raleigh Studios, 600 Chestlehurst Rd. Senoia, GA

Episodes of "The Prison":

- S3E1: "Seed"
- S3E2: "Sick"
- S3E4: "Killer Within"
- S3E5: "Say the Word"
- S3E6: "Hounded"
- S3E7: "When the Dead Come Knocking"
- S3E8: "Made to Suffer"
- S3E9: "The Suicide King"
- S3E10: "Home"
- S3E11: "I Ain't a Judas"
- S3E13: "Arrow on the Doorpost"
- S3E14: "Prey"
- S3E15: "This Sorrowful Life"
- S3E16: "Welcome to the Tombs"
- S4E1: "30 Days Without an Accident"
- S4E2: "Infected"
- S4E3: "Isolation"
- S4E4: "Indifference"
- S5E5: "Internment"
- S4E8: "Too Far Gone"
- S4E9: "After"
- S4E10: "Inmates"

*Originally, the prison was going to be built in Grantville, GA, unfortunately, the day that AMC came to view the property, the train ran every 15 minutes and they decided to spend more money to build it at Raleigh Studios.

**Many scenes from seasons 3-4 were filmed at Raleigh Studio's, including the prison. The studio is private property and a restricted area. At this time and date, it is preferred not to attempt to go on or near studio property.

***The first time Michonne ever shot a gun on the show was when the Governor attacked the prison.

•S4E7: "Dead Weight"

The Governor is walking through the woods along with Martinez, Mitch, and Pete go out looking for supplies, the Governor pauses to look out over the lake and sees a dock. Later in the episode he dumps Pete's body.

•S5E1 "No Sanctuary"

Carol and Tyreese take a Termanite (Martin) captive while Carol goes in search of the group, to save them from Terminus. Martin breaks free and threatens to kill Judith, ordering Tyreese outside to face walkers that are trying to get into the cabin. Tyreese fights off the walkers and saves Judith. When Carol returns, he tells her that Martin is dead.

•S5: Father Gabriel's Church

Episodes of Father Gabriel's Church:

•S5E2: Stranger's
•S5E3: Four Walls and a Roof
•S5E7: Crossed

Father Gabriel's Church was on built on studio property. Production felt due to the graphic and brutalness of the scene, using a real church was unethical.

•S5E14: "Spend"

Abraham is working on a construction team to help expand the wall in Alexandria. Walkers invade the construction site and the Alexandrians show how weak they are and Abraham is forced to kill all the walkers.

Season 6: Hilltop

600 Chestlehurst, Senoia, GA

•S6E11 "Knots Untie"

Jesus brings Ricks group to negotiate for some food and supplies. Rick decides Maggie would be a better negotiator after he meets with Gregory. A fight ensues with some of the Hilltop residents and Rick brutally stabs Ethan after he had stabbed Gregory in the gut.

Season 6: Episode 16: Negan Introduction: "Last Day on Earth"

600 Chestlehurt, Senoia, GA

The group tries to walk Maggie through the woods to get her help when suddendly floodlights flash upon them and they are greeted by Saviors. Negan steps out of the RV and makes the group line-up as he decides which one to kill.

47

7. Season 3-4: Woodbury
Main St, Senoia, GA

Episodes of "Woodbury":

- **S3E3: "Walk With Me"**
- **S3E4: "Killer Within"**
- **S3E5: "Say the Word"**
- **S3E6: "Hounded"**
- **S3E7: "When the Dead Come Knocking"**
- **S3E8: "Made to Suffer"**
- **S3E9: "The Suicide King"**
- **S3E10: "Home"**
- **S3E11: "I Ain't a Judas"**
- **S3E13: "Arrow on the Doorpost"**
- **S3E14: "Prey"**
- **S3E16: "Welcome to the Tombs"**
- **S4E6: "Live Bait"**
- **S4E16: "A"**

In season 3 the governor entices Andrea with his "safe haven" of Woodbury. Michonne of course sees straight through the governor and eventually leaves. Throughout the season, we find that the governor is exactly what Michonne thought, evil!

The Woodbury Town Hall that once occupied Main Street in Senoia was burned down in episode 7, season 4 of The Walking Dead. It was never an actual building; it was a prop that was built just for filming purposes.

*The walker that Andrea shoots in the head in episode 10 was actually played by Special Affect Artist, Greg Nicotero. Greg has played a few memorable walkers throughout the seasons such as the walker that bit Amy, the Deer Walker and Woodbury Walker.

**When a walker bites a character, a blood bag is used covered by a piece of meat to make it look real on camera.

***In "I Ain't Judas", an animatronic walker was used. The walker was used continuously as a replacement for a live walker.

8. Season 3: Milton's Lab/Governor Military Headquarters
Season 6: Episode 2: Enid's Parents: "JSS"
Travis St, Senoia, GA

*Some scenes were also filmed in conjunction with Raleigh Studios.

- **S3E3 "Walk With Me"**

Milton's Lab

•S3E7 "When the Dead Come Knocking"
Maggie and Glenn are held hostage

Milton's Lab

•S3E8 "Made to Suffer"
Glenn and Maggie escape

•S3E10 "Home"
Milton's Lab

•S3E14 "Prey"
Governor's torture chamber

Milton shows Andrea

Andrea is tied up

Martinez tells the Governor about the charred walkers

•S3E16 "Welcome to the Tombs"
Milton turns

Andrea dies

•S6E2: "JSS"
(Beside rock wall building)

Enid's parents are eaten by walkers while Enid watches in the vehicle.

9. Season 3: Episode 7: Abandoned Cabin: "When the Dead Come Knocking"

Hwy 85, Senoia, GA

Rick, Daryl, Oscar and Michonne head to Woodbury. As they're walking through the woods they're forced into a small cabin by walkers where they find an old man asleep and have to find a way out of the cabin besieged by walkers.

10. Season 3: Episode 15: Merle's Last Drink: "This Sorrowful Life"

Southern Country Steakhouse – "Jake's Bar" 34 Chestlehurst Rd, Senoia, GA

Merle has just set Michonne free and he is having his last drink. He leaves this area and heads to the ambush site in Haralson, GA.

11. Season 4: Episode 4: Dead Battery: "Indifference"

1226 Johnson Rd, Senoia, GA (On the corner of Johnson and Deep South Rd)

Daryl, Michonne, Bob and Tyreese find a new car but the battery is dead. Tyreese intentionally gets overrun by a walker and Michonne gets mad at him telling him his anger will get him killed. Bob confides in Daryl about his alcoholism.

12. Season 4: Episode 7: Old Cabin: "Dead Weight"

Hwy 85, Senoia, GA

The Governor, Martinez, Pete, and Mitch are walking through the woods looking for an old cabin that may have supplies. They find the cabin after following a trail of headless bodies.

13. Season 4: Episode 9: Carl Escapes Walkers: "After"

258 Pylant St. Senoia, GA

Carl goes out on his own and barely escapes 3 walkers while Rick is recovering at the claimed house.

14. Season 4: Episode 11: Carl and Michonne Search for Food: "Claimed"

210 Pylant St. Senoia, GA

Rick is recovering and Michonne and Carl go searching for food. When they cannot find food in this house, they move onto the next one.

15. Season 4 Episode 11: Michonne Finds Bodies: "Claimed"

220 Pylant St. Senoia, GA

Michonne and Carl enter this house where Michonne finds bodies in a room and then lies to Carl about what she has found.

16. Season 4: Episode 9 and 11: Claimed House: "After" and "Claimed"
291 Pylant St, Senoia, GA

•S4E9 "After"

Rick and Carl find a house and take refuge. Rick has fallen into a deep sleep due to his injuries. Carl tried to wake him up but can't and comes to the conclusion that his father is dead. When Rick finally awakens, he tells Carl he is proud of him for getting supplies and that he is a man now. Later in the episode, Michonne finds the house and is happy to be reunited with them.

•S4E11 "Claimed"

Rick hears a commotion in the house and is startled by men entering the house. Rick hides as he hears the group of men torturing one of their members. As Rick hears footsteps coming up the stairs, he hides under the bed as the man enters the room and drops on the bed and falls asleep.

After Len knocks out Tony and Rick can escape from under the bed, Rick hears the men trying to stake "claimed" on Michonne. Rick runs to the restroom where he finds one of the survivors using the toilet. Rick strangles the man.

*The scenes from the bathroom were filmed on set at Raleigh Studios

17. Season 4: Episode 4: Michonne's Flashback: "After"
Southern Living Home, 57 Morgan St, Senoia, GA 30276

Michonne has fallen asleep and dreams of her happy life with her baby boy and her boyfriend Mike and his friend Terry. As the dream goes on, it turns into an utter nightmare when she sees the two with their arms cut off like in the post-apocalyptic world she has come to know.

18. Season 4: Episode 4: The Pudding House: "After"
239 Pylant St, Senoia, GA

Carl goes on a supply run; he finds what is now known as "The Pudding House". He finds a walker in the bedroom and almost gets bitten but gets away and leaves his shoe behind. When he gets downstairs, he finds a large can of pudding, and sits on the roof and eats the entire can.

19. Season 4: Episode 10 and 15: The Bridge and Tunnel: "Inmates" and "Us"
Travis St. (Railroad Tracks) Senoia, GA

•S4E10 "Inmates"
Tyreese, Carol, Lizzie, and Mika find a "Terminus" sign. They walk the tracks towards the bridge.

•S4E15 "Us"
While following after Maggie and her group, Glenn and Tara decide to enter the tunnel, while Eugene, Rosita, and Abraham decide to go around finding a different way to the other side of the tunnel.

*The entrance to the bridge / tunnel was made up to look like concrete. Then CGI was used in this episode to hide the bridge above.

**The interior tunnel scenes were filmed at Raleigh Studios.

20. Season 4: Episode 11: Rick, Michonne and Carl find Terminus Sign: "Claimed"

Andrews Pkwy and Pylant St, Senoia, GA

As Rick, Michonne and Carl leave the "Claimed House" they see a sign baring the words, "Sanctuary for All. Community for All. Those who arrive, Survive." They take directions and continue walking.

21. Season 4: Episode 13: Bob's Backstory: "Alone"
Season 5: Episode 2: Daryl and Carol Search for Beth: "Strangers"
Season 5: Episode 10: Flare Walker: "Them"
Season 6: Episode 2: Enid Eats Turtle: "JSS"
Season 6: Episode 3: Rick Cut's Hand: "Thank You"
Season 6: Episode 10: Rick and Daryl Leave Jesus "Start to Finish"

Crook Rd, Senoia, GA

•S4E13 "Alone"

Bob is lying on top of a truck and Daryl pulls up and asks him the three famous questions. "How many walkers have you killed? How many people have you killed? Why?" Bob questions if they have a camp and goes with Daryl to join the group.

*Crook Rd has been used in many episodes of TWD. Many driving scenes were filmed here most likely because of its close proximity to Raleigh Studios.

**Crook Rd was referenced in Season 4 Episode 11"Claimed" when Abraham was driving right before him and Tara cleared the road. Tara wrote, "Crook with Balloon" on her hand.

***During filming of Season 5, the crew had changed the name of Crook Rd to Tom Luse Pkwy. Tom Luse of course is one of the Executive Producers of the show.

Please respect owners wishes: DO NOT TRESPASS ON ANY PROPERTY!!!

54

•S5E2: "Strangers"

Carol tries to leave and Daryl goes after her. Then he spots the car with the cross and jumps in another car after in search for Beth.

•S5E10: "Them"

Rick heads in a different direction than what Aaron tells him, they run down walkers and the car stops running. When they leave the car, they are left fighting walkers in the woods where they shoot a flare gun into the eye of a walker.

•S6E2: "JSS"

Enid has escaped walkers after her parents were eaten and looking for safety, Enid finds a turtle that she kills for food. She then uses the bones to write JSS which stands for "just survive somehow".

•S36E3: "Thank You"

When Rick is running back to the RV, he runs down the road killing walkers and accidently cuts his hand with a knife he just used to kill a zombie.

•S6E10: "Start to Finish"

Rick and Daryl find Jesus changing the tire of the food truck he had stolen from them, tie him up and steal it back.

*The scene with Michonne and Spencer where they find Walker Deanna were filmed in the woods near Crook Rd. This is considered studio property and should not be trespassed upon.

22. Season 4: Episode 16: The Train Car: "A"

Travis St, Senoia, GA

Scenes from the train car from the season finale were filmed in a train car on the tracks in Senoia. Fans watched as Andrew Lincoln jumped up and down and pounded the ground to get into character for this intense final scene of Season 4.

23. Season 5: Episode 5: Bus Crash: "Self Help"

Dolly Nixon Rd, Senoia, GA

Eugene causes bus crash to keep group from advancing to Washington D.C.

24. Season 5: Episodes 5 and 7: Fire Truck Breaks Down and Eugene Knocked Out: "Self Help" and "Crossed"

Rock House Rd, Senoia, GA (Off Rockhouse and Crawford)

The fire truck breaks down and Abraham starts leading Eugene towards a large group of walkers. The others in the group try to stop Abraham and

Eugene blurts out that he is a fake and does not have the cure. Abraham knocks Eugene out cold.

25. Season 5: Episode 10: RV Breaks Down: "The Distance"
Dolly Nixon Rd, Senoia, GA

The group is headed for Washington DC when the RV's battery dies; Glenn fixes the battery thanks to what Dale taught him.

26. Season 5: Run Down House and Barn
Dolly Nixon, Senoia, GA

•S5E11: "The Distance"
Rick hides flare gun in a blender.

•S5E12: "Remember"
(Barn) Rick decides not to kill a walker that walks out of the barn. (House) Rick returns to find that the gun is missing from the blender. Rick and Carl have a talk. Carl kills walker that comes from under the blanket.

•S5E13: "Forget
Rick, Daryl and Carol have a talk and find a walker with a "W" on its forehead

27. Seasons 5 & 6: "Alexandria"
Gin Street, Senoia, GA

Alexandria "Safe Zone" is where Aaron leads Rick and his group. When the group arrives they do not know how to act in "normal civilization."

Episodes of Alexandria:

- •S5E12 "The Distance"
- •S5E13 "Forget"
- •S5E14 "Spend"
- •S5E15 "Try"
- •S5E16 "Conquer"
- •S6E1 "First Time Again"
- •S6E2 "JSS"
- •S6E4 "Here's Not Here"
- •S6E5 "Now"
- •S6E7 "Heads Up"
- •S6E8 "Start to Finish"
- •S6E9 "No Way Out"
- •S6E10 "The Next World"
- •S6E11 "Knots Untie"
- •S6E12 "Not Tomorrow Yet"
- •S6E14 "Twice As Far"
- •S6E16 "Last Day on Earth"

Haralson

Welcome to Haralson, GA

Haralson is a small farming community whom is best known for its Empire Cotton Seed in the early to mid-20th century.

Their film history started in 1975 with the movie Moonrunners which was the pilot to The Dukes of Hazard. In the years to follow, such movies as, The War, Fried Green Tomatoes, Driving Miss Daisy, Pet Cemetery II, The Unseen and Mama Flores Family were all filmed here in the 90's with a total of 10 major movies have been shot there.

A short time after, Dolly Parton and Queen Latifah paid a visit while filming Joyful Noise, then Shia LeBeouf while filming Lawless (2012). Scenes from Footloose (2011) were shot inside the Old Thompson Mercantile building from the dance. Then in 2012, The Walking Dead came knocking at our door. To date, there have been a total of 22 episodes filmed in and around the Haralson area.

Walkin Dead Tours and Events

Interested in a tour of Haralson locations, contact us at 678-329-4400 or www.walkindeadharalson.com or visit us on Facebook or at www.walkindead haralson.com. Don't forget to check out the gift shop, Cherokee Rose with a wide variety of custom made items by fans and for fans of TWD. Cherokee Rose 10 Line Creek Rd, Haralson, GA.

1. Opening Credits: Esco Feed Mill
Line Creek Rd., Haralson, GA

The Esco Feed Mill has been featured in every opening credit in Season 3-4.

2. Season 2: Episode 9: Lori's Accident: "Triggerfinger"
Aaron Todd Rd, Haralson, GA

Lori flips her car and is knocked out in her accident and wakes up having to fight off walkers.

3. Season 2: Episode 14: Rick and Glenn Look for Hershel: "Nebraska"
Main St, Haralson, GA

Rick and Glenn are looking for Hershel at the bar and drive through town.

4. Opening Credits: Thompson Mercantile
Season 3: Episode 1: Michonne Gets Aspirin for Andrea: "Seed"
32 Main St, Haralson, GA

This building has been used in a few scenes in the show including every opening credit of season 3-4 and in the episode "Seed". Michonne enters this store to retrieve some aspirin for Andrea.

5. Season 3: Episode 1: Andrea and Michonne's Safe Haven: "Seed"
Sportsman Deer Cooler 34 Addy St GA 74/85, Haralson, GA

Michonne and Andrea spent the winter here, now Andrea has taken sick. Michonne is trying to get her better. They decide to move and exit out the back door with Michonne's pets in tow through the woods.

6. Season 3: Episode 3: Andrea and Michonne See Helicopter Crash Site: "Walk With Me"
515 Line Creek Rd., Haralson, GA

Andrea, Michonne and pets discover a smoke from a crash and walk into the field to investigate.

*The actual helicopter crash location was located on the Raleigh Studios property in Senoia, GA.

7. Seasons 3-4: Episode S3E3 and S4E6: Governor Military Ambush/ Walker Falls in Campfire: "Walk With Me" and "Live Bait"
Rising Star Rd., Haralson, GA

•S3E3 "Walk With Me"
The Governor approaches the National Guards men with white flags flying. He swears he comes in peace but prepares to ambush the men and steals all the supplies and vehicles and takes them back to Woodbury where he lies to his people about how he attained them.

•S4E6 "Live Bait"
After the Governor falls from grace, he is feeling sorry for himself in front of a campfire as a walker approaches him and falls into the fire. Martinez, who is obviously tired of his behavior, walks up and shoots the walker in the head.

*See the fire ring in Cherokee Rose.

8. Season 3: Episode 7: Search for Maggie and Glenn: "When the Dead Come Knocking" & Season 5: Episode 10: Maggie Kills Walker in Tree: "Them"
Fox Hollow Rd, Haralson, GA

•S3E7: "When the Dead Come Knocking"
Rick, Michonne, Daryl and Oscar go looking for Maggie and Glenn and walk down a dirt path.

•S5E10: "Them"
Maggie is mourning the loss of Beth next to a tree, a walker comes up behind her and she kills it.

9. Season 3: Episode 9: Merle's Return to Group & Maggie, Glenn and Rick Fight: "The Suicide King"

Dead Oak Rd, Haralson, GA

•S3E9: "The Suicide King"

Rick, Daryl, Maggie, Michonne and Glenn argue about Merle's return to the group. Daryl and Merle leave group.

•S3E9: "The Suicide King"

Maggie, Glenn and Rick stop to move a red truck. Glenn stomps on a walkers head repeatedly because he is upset that Rick didn't kill the Governor for almost raping Maggie but saved Daryl and Merle instead.

10. Season 3: Episode 13: Hershel Parks Car: "Arrow on the Doorpost"

Railroad St, Haralson, GA

Hershel pulls up to the complex and lets Rick out of the car. Hershel checks his gun to make sure it's secure.

11. Season 3: Episode 13: Daryl and Rick Enter Complex: "Arrow on the Doorpost"

Railroad St, Haralson, GA

Rick and Daryl enter the silo complex and start scoping out the location in case of an attack.

12. Season 3: Episode 13: The Move In: "Arrow on the Doorpost"

Magnolia St, Haralson, GA

Rick and Daryl move toward the meeting barn and secure the area.

13. Season 3: Episode 13: The Meeting Barn: "Arrow on the Doorpost"

Main St, Haralson, GA

Rick skeptically confronts the Governor and discusses possible attacks on the prison and the group. The Governor offers Rick some whiskey and tells him his story of losing his wife. After a long discussion, the Governor asks Rick to offer up Michonne instead of him ambushing the entire group in a full, blown out war.

*See Rick and the Governor's chairs along with several other props from this scene inside Cherokee Rose Retail.

14. Season 3: Episode 13: Walker Kills: "Arrow on the Doorpost"
Railroad St, Haralson, GA

Martinez and Daryl have a competition on who can kill walkers better. Andrea gets tired of their behavior and starts stabbing walkers in the head.

15. Season 3: Episode 15: Merle Enters Complex: "This Sorrowful Life"
Line Creek Rd, Haralson, GA

Merle enters the complex with his music blaring with walkers following behind him. He jumps out of the car and approaches the silo complex and enters the back of the barn.

*During filming of "A Sorrowful Life", there were over 50 walkers on the set. The walkers even attacked a bus load of school kids that afternoon. The kids thought it was cool!

16. Season 3: Episode 15: The Barn: "This Sorrowful Life"
Railroad St, Haralson, GA

Merle enters the barn and goes to the window and starts shooting at the Governor and all his men. A walker attacks Merle, they exit then he kills the walker and he and Martinez fight and the Governor steps in to finish the job.

The Governor takes Merle back into the barn to finish him off. He bites off his pinky and ring finger and spits them out. He lifts his gun and kills Merle.

17. Season 3: Episode 15: Daryl Finds Merle: "This Sorrowful Life"
Railroad St, Haralson, GA

Daryl walks up and sees Walker Merle eating Ben. Merle gets up and goes towards Daryl and Daryl attacks him, stabbing him repeatedly in the face. Daryl falls back and cries.

18. Season 3: Episode 16: Governor Kills His People: "Welcome to the Tombs"
Grey Girls Rd, Haralson, GA

The governor freaks out and kills all of his men except one. Rick and Daryl find her on their way to Woodbury after the Governor attacks the prison.

19. Season 4: Episode 11: Glenn and Abraham Fight: "Claimed"
Line Creek and Grey Girls Rd, Haralson, GA

Glenn wakes up to find himself in the back of a military truck. He beats on the back window until Abraham gets bad and stops the truck. Glenn wants to search for Maggie but Abraham is insistent on getting Dr. Eugene Porter to Washington D.C. because he believes he has "the cure" to what is causing people to turn. Abraham insists that Maggie is dead and Glenn punches him in the face. The two start fighting and Tara and Rosita try to break up the fight.

Eugene sees walkers coming out of the field and tries to kill them, opening fire on the truck, piercing holes in the gas tank. As the group reassembles, Glenn goes off in search of Maggie and the group follows behind him.

20. Season 5: Episode 10: Father Gabriel Talks to Maggie "Them"
Rowe Rd, Haralson, GA

Father Gabriel tells Maggie that he would pray for her family. Maggie said she doesn't need his prayer.

21. Season 5: Episode 10: Sasha Kills Dogs for Food: "Them"
Dead Oak Rd, Haralson, GA

The group is starving, meanwhile a pack of dogs come through the woods so Sasha kills them for food.

22. Season 5: Episode 10: Maggie Finds Walker in Trunk: "Them"
Dead Oak Rd, Haralson, GA

Maggie looks in the trunk of a car for food and water and finds a walker. She closes the trunk and can't get it back open. Glenn opens the trunk and kills the walker.

23. Season 5: Episode 10: The Group Finds Vehicles: "Them" & Season 6: Episode 16: The Group's First Run In With The Saviors: "Last Day On Earth"
Sullivan Mill Rd, Haralson, GA

•S5E10: "Them

Aaron tells the group where to find the vehicles. Abraham and the group goes searching for them and finds Eric in the process

•S6E16: "Last Day On Earth"

The group tries to get Maggie to Hilltop for medical attention and was road blocked by the Saviors.

24. Season 6: Episodes 1 & 3: Walkers Invade Alexandria "First Time Again" & "Thank You"

Crossroads of Gordon and Glazier Rd/Eastside School Rd, Haralson, GA

Rick finds out the trap (quarry) that keeps walkers from invading Alexandria is about to fail. He conducts a plan to keep them in. They build a wall on Redding and Marshall, which was actually on the corner of Gordon and Glazier.

25. Season 6: Episode 8: Introduction to Negan: "No Way Out"
Eastside School Rd, Haralson, GA

Daryl, Sasha and Abraham are driving back to Alexandria after acquiring a new vehicle and are stopped by a motorcycle gang. They inform them to hand over all their belongings because they now belong to Negan.

26. Season 6: Episode 15: Rick and Morgan Look for Carol: "East"
Al Roberts Rd, Haralson, GA

As Rick and Morgan look for Carol, they end up finding a walker instead. Morgan reveals to Rick that he had one of the wolves locked up in Alexandria. Rick then reveals to Morgan that Michonne ate his protein bar.

Gay

1. Season 3: Episode 6: Merle finds Maggie and Glenn: "Hounded"

Runyan Automotive, 20315 State Route 85, Luthersville Rd., Gay, GA

Maggie and Glenn are on a run for formula for Judith. Merle comes from around the corner and finds the two and takes them hostage. Michonne is lurking in the shadows and she picks up for formula and goes searching for "the prison".

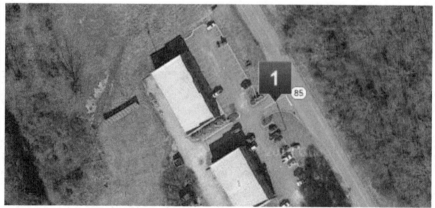

2. Season 6: Episode 3: Daryl Lures Walkers: "Thank You"

Flat Shoals Rd, Gay, GA

Daryl is seen overhead riding his motorcycle, to meet back with Abraham and Sasha to continue to lead walkers away from Alexandria.

*Season 6 was the first time production used drones for overhead shots.

3. Season 6: Episode 4: Morgan: "Here's Not Here"
Flat Shoals Rd on Flint River, Gay, GA

Morgan's flashback of after he left King County, he comes across Eastman, a man that has been surviving by himself in the apocalypse with his beloved goat Tabitha. Eastman teaches Morgan the art of aikido. As the episode progresses, Eastman is bitten by a walker and Tabitha is also eaten, once again leaving Morgan alone.

The home that was used in the filming of this episode is a private residence. They do not wish to be disturbed therefore; it was not listed or mapped in this book.

Please respect the owner's wishes and do not attempt to locate this property.

Woodbury

1. Season 4: Episode 9: Rick and Carl Food Search: "After"
Riverside Inn, 29 River Cove Rd, Woodbury, GA

Rick and Carl find this abandoned diner that is barricaded, Rick tries to kill the walker inside with an axe but is weak from his injuries inflicted by the Governor. He has Carl shoot the walker in the head and they continue to search for food.

2. Season 6 Episode 12: Rick Makes a Stop: "Not Tomorrow Yet"
Cove Rd, Woodbury, GA

Rick makes a stop to go over the attack on the Saviors before going to the satellites.

3. Season 6: Episode 12: The Satellite Dishes: "Not Tomorrow Yet"
Cove Rd, Woodbury, GA

The group arrives at these large satellite dishes in hopes to kill Negan by going room by room killing everyone in their path. Glenn finds a room with

Polaroid's where he sees brutally killed people with their heads crushed. They end up in a stand-off by early morning while Maggie and Carol are taken hostage by the Saviors.

4. Season 6: Episode 15: Carol Kills Saviors: "East"
River Cove Rd, Woodbury, GA

Carol kills some of the Saviors after they shoot out her car tires. One of the Saviors follows Carol into the woods.

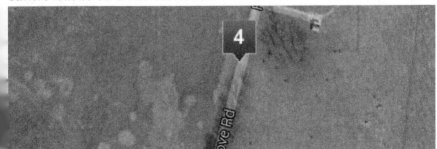

Manchester

1. Season 6: Episode 1: Luring Walkers: "First Time Again"

Old Chevrolet Dealership, Truitt St and Mcclain Rd, Manchester, GA

Glenn, Nicholas and Heath were sent to kill the walkers in the store so their noisy banging on the windows would not throw the herd off course. The walkers break through the windows and almost kill the three men.

1. Season 4: Episode 8: The Governor Leaves Lilly and Meaghan: "Too Far Gone"

Sprewell Bluff State Park, 740 Sprewell Bluff Rd, Thomaston GA

Lilly and Meaghan are left at camp while the governor's crew tries to take over the prison. Meghan is busy playing and a walker comes up out of the ground and viciously attacks her.

Milner

1. Season 4: Episode 14: Look at the flowers: "The Grove"
Green Wood St, Milner, GA

As Tyreese, Carol, Judith, Mika and Lizzie continue their journey to Terminus; they come across a house in a grove. Carol thinks it's a good idea that they stay and rest a few days.

While in the house, Carol spots Lizzie out in the yard playing with a walker and rushed outside to kill it. Lizzie is of course upset with Carol and screams that she killed her friend. After a couple days, they find Lizzie in the yard with a lifeless Mika. Lizzie assures Carol and Tyreese that Mika is okay because she didn't stab her in the brain. The following morning, Carol takes Lizzie out to the grove and tells her to, "look at the flowers" and kills her knowing that she was a threat to them all. Later that evening, Carol tells Tyreese that she was responsible for killing David and Karen. Tyreese forgives her and they continue on with their journey.

Owners of "The Grove" do not wish to disclose the address of their property. Please do not trespass!!!

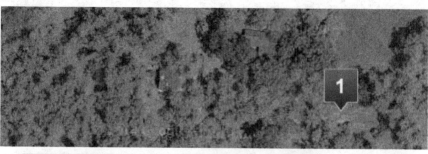

Please respect owners wishes: DO NOT TRESPASS ON ANY PROPERTY!!!

1. Season 4: Episode 6: Brian Heriot Barn: "Live Bait"

1495 Rover Zetella Road, Williamson, GA

The Governor is searching and is lost after falling from his power. He wanders around and comes across a barn with the name "Brian Heriot" on it. He later takes the name on and refers to himself by that name to Lilly and her family.

2. Season 4: Episode 6: Camp: "Live Bait"

Rover Zetella Rd, Williamson, GA

The Governor, Lilly, Tara and Meaghan camp out by the lake and the Governor and Lilly have a brief romantic encounter.

3. Season 5: Episodes 11 and 12: Storm Cabin: "The Distance" & "Remember"

IB Howard Rd, Williamson, GA

The group takes shelter to keep safe from a tornado, they all barricade the door to keep walkers from coming in when a tornado hits. The next day, Sasha and Maggie leave the barn and go out and have a talk in a meadow, Aaron appears and says he's a friend. This startles Maggie and Sasha because he knew who Rick was.

Also filmed on this property:
The group is looking for food and Sasha comes across some dead frogs. Daryl eats worms.

Brooks

Season 6: Episode 10: Rick and Daryl Travel to Sorghum Barn: "The Next World"
Line Creek Rd and Fairview Rd, Brooks, GA

Traveling to to get some Sorghum, Rick and Daryl turn this corner.

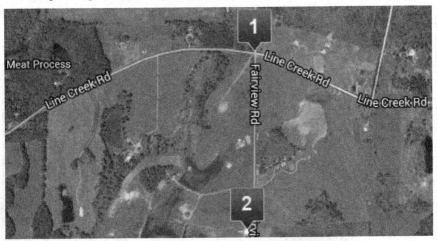

Season 6: Episode 10: Sorghum Barn: "The Next World"
1045 Fairview Rd, Brooks, GA

While out on a run, Rick and Daryl find a supply truck with plenty of food in it in a large red barn with the word Sorghum on the outside of it. Eugene had asked them to look for Sorghum because it would last them for a while and everything would be "hunky dunky".

Griffin

1. Opening Credits: Plantation House
Season 2: Episode 4: Plantation House: "Cherokee Rose"

5157 W Macintosh Rd, Griffin, GA

Daryl goes looking for Sophia and comes across this house. After his search comes up empty, he finds a "Cherokee Rose" on the ground that he decides to take for Carol.

Please respect owners wishes: DO NOT TRESPASS ON ANY PROPERTY!!

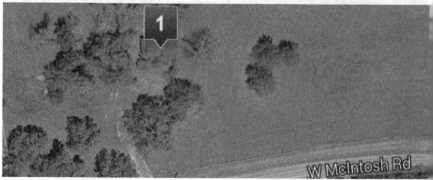

2. Season 2: Episode 10: Rick and Shane Try to Leave Randall: "18 Miles Out"

American Tanning and Leather Company, 730 Pimento Ave, Griffin, GA

Rick and Shane have a confrontation about Lori and Randall is left pleading for his life, as he mentions he knows Maggie from high school. Shane throws a wrench through the window, several walkers exit through the window. Rick saves Randall from the horde and they leave Shane trapped in the school bus. Rick then changes his mind and saves Shane, then puts Randall (tied-up) back into the vehicle.

3. Season 3: Episode 10: Line Creek Bridge: "Home"
Line Creek Bridge, Line Creek Rd (off the dirt road), Griffin, GA

Merle and Daryl are walking through the woods when Daryl hears a baby crying. They come across a bridge with a family fighting walkers and Daryl decides to go help. Merle tries to harass the family and Daryl steps in and gets angry.

4. Season 4: Episode 1: Big Spot: "30 Day Without and Accident"
655 N Expressway, Griffin, GA

Daryl bangs on the front window antagonizing the walkers. Daryl, Tyreese, Glenn, Sasha, Bob and Zack enter the store looking for supplies. Glenn is off looking at baby stuff and finds a camera. Bob is looking at the alcohol when the shelf tips over causing Bob to get stuck. As they figure out how to get Bob released, walkers start falling through the ceiling from the weight of a helicopter crash. While Zack is trying to help Bob get out, he is bitten by a walker and left to be consumed as the group makes a frantic escape.

*All scenes from the inside of "Big Spot" were filmed inside Raleigh Studios in Senoia, GA.

5. Season 4: Episode 4: Rick and Carol's Run: "Indifference"

Waterford Subdivision (Off of West Ellis Rd) Griffin, GA

Rick and Carol go on a run. Rick is concerned with Carol's behavior in how she killed Karen. They run into a couple survivors that later get eaten by walkers. Rick insists Tyreese will kill Carol when he finds out that she killed Karen so he assures her that she is better off on her own and leaves her.

*The inside of the house was filmed at 143 Waterford Way and the outside was filmed at 130 Tuscany.

6. Season 4: Episode 6: Governor Pushes Walker: "Live Bait"

225 Meriwether St. Griffin, GA

The Governor is searching for a safe haven and knocks over a walker in his attempts.

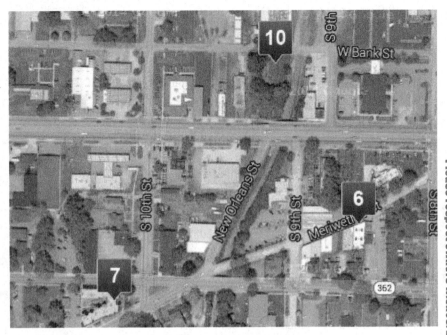

7. Season 4: Episode 6: Lilly's Apartment: "Live Bait"
Marian Point Apartments 416 W Poplar St, Griffin, GA

The Governor approaches a building and sees a small girl that resembles his daughter, Penny. He enters the building and meets Lilly, Tara, Meaghan and their father who has stage 4 Lung Cancer. They feed the Governor Spaghetti O's and let him have a place to sleep and request of him to go get their father an oxygen tank.

*Some scenes may have been filmed at Raleigh Studio

8. Season 4: Episode 12: Beth Looks for a Drink: "Still"
The Club at Shoal Creek, 430 Country Club Dr. Griffin, GA

Beth enters the golf course in search of alcohol because she confides in Daryl that her father never let her have any. Beth finds a bottle of unopened wine, but is forced to smash the bottle as a walker tries to attack her. As they make their way through the club house, Beth finds a bottle of Peach Schnapps and Daryl smashes it on the ground and tells her that her first drink needs to be something better.

9. Season 4: Episode 15: Glenn Finds a Sign and Abraham's Army Looks for Glenn: "Us"

520-612 Pimento Ave, Griffin, GA

Glenn finds a sign from Maggie and takes off running, Abraham, Tara, Rosita and Eugene go chasing after him.

Later in the episode, Abraham, Rosita and Eugene go looking for Glenn in the minivan.

10. Season 4: Episode 15: Auto Shop: "Us"

165 W Banks St, Griffin, GA

Daryl wakes up to Len accusing him of stealing his rabbit. The group later finds out that Len is lying and beats him to death. As they leave, Daryl sees Len's body wrapped in a sheet with an arrow in his head.

* The railroad tracks they walk are located next to the shop.

11. Season 5: Episode 2: Gun Shop: "Stranger's"

127 Slaton Avenue, Griffin, GA

Glenn, Maggie and Tara are looking for supplies; Glenn enters the gun shop where he finds some silencers in an old freezer.

12. Season 5: Episode 2: Food Bank: "Stranger's"

109 Slaton Avenue, Griffin, GA

Father Gabriel escorts the group to a food bank; which was once supported by his church. While there, he is terrified when he sees the walker that was formerly his wife. This is also where Bob was bitten.

*Map shows path they walked to Food Bank.

13. Season 5: Episode 2: Bob's Leg: "Stranger's"
502 N. Hill St, Griffin, GA

After the Termites kidnap Bob, they remove the lower part of his leg and cook it at this location; not knowing he had been bitten.

*This was also used in scenes with Father Gabriel and Morgan S5E8.

14. Season 5: Episode 5: Book Store and Abraham's Flashbacks: "Self Help"
Easy Shop, 375 North 13th Street, Griffin, GA

Abraham and his group take refuge for the evening. Abraham and Rosita partake in some love making while Eugene watches from the "Self Help" section of the book store.

*Scenes from Abraham's flashbacks including when he met Eugene and his breakdown were filmed on the side and in the parking lot of the Easy Shop.

15. Season 5: Episode 5: Fire Department: "Self Help"

102 North Sixth St, Griffin, GA

Abraham's group acquires a fire truck and Eugene kills a horde of walkers with the fire hose.

16. Season 5: Episode 6: Battered Women's Shelter: "Consumed"

Whalen Law Offices, 100 South Hill Street Suite 524, Griffin, GA

Daryl and Carol take refuge in Battered Women's Shelter for the evening. Carol sees a child turned walker through the window and Daryl takes care of it for her.

*Behind this building is where Daryl and Noah take the truck State Alley and Solomon St. In front of the building is where Daryl and Carol see the Grady car on W Solomon and 8th Street.

17. Season 5: Episode 7: Sasha Gets Knocked Out: "Crossed"

502 W Broadway, Griffin, GA

The group is looking for Beth and Carol. They make plans at this old warehouse set in Atlanta. Sasha believes one of the captives and he knocks her out so he can escape.

18. Season 5: Episode 14: Solar Plant: "Spend"
Old Nacom Building, 375 Airport Road, Griffin, GA

A group heads out to find solar parts to fix the power grid in Alexandria. While they are gone, Aiden shoots at a walker that has a grenade attached to it. An explosion goes off that hurts Aiden and Tara. Aiden eventually dies while the rest of the group tried to escape. Noah is killed while trying to get out.

19. Season 5: Episode 16: Old Mill: "Conquer"
Off Rehoboth Rd and 6th St on Searcy Ave, Griffin, GA

Aaron and Daryl are in search of good people for Alexandria when they come across an old mill with food trucks. They get to the safety of a car when they find out that it's all a trap, set up by the wolves. Morgan appears and saves them and they take Morgan back to Alexandria.

20. Season 6: Episode 6: Abraham on the Bridge: "Always Accountable"

Sixth Street Bridge, Griffin, GA

Abraham spots a Humvee on an abandonded bridge where he also spots a walker with a rocket launcher. After fighting with the walker, Abraham goes back to the Humvee and smokes a cigar where he sees the walker slip through the bar it is impaled on and slip to the ground. He then retrieves the rocket launcher.

21. Season 6: Episode 6: Abraham and Sasha Hide Out: "Always Accountable"

East Broad St near Sixth Street Bridge, Griffin, GA

Abraham and Sasha hide out while waiting for Daryl to back track to them. Abraham hits on Sasha.

22. Season 6: Episode 6: Chase from the Saviors: "Always Accountable"

High Falls Rd, Griffin, GA

Daryl, Abraham and Sasha try to escape the Saviors and race down this road. The run into some Saviors and Daryl crashes his motorcycle.

23. Season 6: Episode 10: Rick and Daryl Meet Jesus: "The Next Word"
2687 High Falls Rd, Griffin, GA

Rick and Daryl stop at an old gas station where they run into a man that refers to himself as Jesus. Jesus tricks Rick and Daryl with firecrackers as he steals their truck.

24. Season 6: Episode 11: The Search for Jesus' People: "Knots Untie"
839 Everee Inn Rd. Griffin, GA

After coming across a recent accident; Jesus claims that the people in the wreck were some of his people. The group locates some of them in a building and rescues them from walkers. Abraham accidently confuses Freddie for a walker and almost kills him.

25. Season 6: Episode 14: Roadblock: "Twice As Far"

Pimento Ave. Griffin, GA

Daryl, Rosita and Denise get stopped at this location when a tree falls in the road.

26. Season 6: Episode 14: Edison Apothecary: "Twice As Far"

462 W Solomon St, Griffin, GA

Daryl, Rosita and Denise arrive at the drugstore where they raid the shelves. Denise finds a walker that is trapped and a blood filled sink with the body of a possible child.

27. Season 6: Episode 14: Path to Drug Store: "Twice As Far"

West College Street, Griffin, GA

Daryl, Rosita and Denise walk this path to the drugstore. Rosita meets up with them in the middle.

28. Season 6: Episode 14: Eugene's Machine Shop: "Twice As Far"

Woodruff Dr, Griffin, GA

Eugene takes Abraham to a machine shop where he tells him he is going to produce ammunition. A walker covered in metal approaches him and he is unable to kill it leaving Abraham to do the job.

29. Season 6: Episode 14: "Twice As Far"
On railroad tracks off of Carver and Kalamazoo Dr. Griffin, GA

- •Denise finds soda
- •Denise Dies
- •Rosita, Glenn and Michonne look for Daryl

30. Season 6: Episode 16: Morgan on Horse: "Last Day on Earth"
East Broad St, Griffin, GA

Morgan goes out on horseback in hopes of finding Carol.

31. Season 6: Episode16: Morgan Finds Carol: "Last Day on Earth"
Spalding County Extension Service, 222 East Broad St, Griffin, GA

Morgan finds Carol hurt at this location. He tries to reason with her to come back to the group and she tells Morgan that she wants to be on her own.

32. Season 6: Episode 16: Savior Shoots Carol: "Last Day on Earth"
East Broadway and N. Hill St. Griffin, GA

As Carol tries to run away from Morgan, she comes across the last surviving Savior that she attempted to kill. He shoots her in the arm and leg in attempts to watch her die until Morgan shows up and kills the Savior. Two men in armor appear and help Morgan and Carol.

Walkin DEAD Hampton

Enjoy touring the scenes from The Walking Dead Season 6 episodes 3 and 7. Find out where Glenn escaped death and where Michonne and the group hid out in the pet store. Start off at the Speakeasy Bookstore and go with a guide for the entire experience.

1. Season 2: Episode 1 & 2: Highway Disaster: "What Lies Ahead" & "Bloodletting"

GA-20 W near Atlanta Motor Speedway

The group is headed towards Ft. Benning when the radiator hose bursts on Dale's RV; they're forced to stop for repairs and to clear the road. A horde of walkers come passing though and Andrea gets stuck in the trailer to battle the infamous RV Walker. As the horde passes through, Rick and Sophia enter the woods where Rick tells Sophia to stay put, later to find she has gone missing.

2. Season 6: Episode 3: The Group Enters Town: "Thank You"
Main St, Hampton, GA

The group comes across an abandonded town where Nicholas leads the group to various locations in the town despite having either some PTSD or flashbacks. They enter the town towards an old gas station and proceed from there.

3. Season 6: Episode 3:Found Sturgis: "Thank You"
Cherry St, Hampton, GA

Nicholas finds that his friend Sturgis has been eaten.

4. Season 6: Episode 3: Pet Shop: "Thank You"
14 Main St, Hampton, GA

Michonne and Heath argue about the group splitting up. Michonne insists to Heath that the group must stay together for the safelty of the whole group. David writes a letter to his wife in the meantime and Michonne writes on her arm telling David that he will make it home.

92

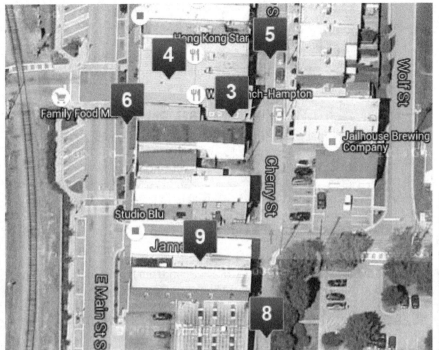

5. Season 6: Episode 3: Nicholas Kills Walker: "Thank You"
Cherry St, Hampton, GA

Glenn and Nicholas come across a walker that was a part of Nicholas' tour in the past. Glenn tried to convince Nicholas that he is not the same person anymore.

6. Season 6: Episode 3: Annie is Eaten: "Thank You"
Main St, Hampton, GA

As the group tries to escape from the pet shop, Annie falls and the rest of the group is unable to save her from a hoard of walkers.

7. Season 6: Episode 3: David is Eaten: "Thank You"
Main St, and Barrett St

Trying to escape the town, the group comes to a gate and tries to jump over it. David is sadly eaten by walkers while the others make it over safely.

8. Season 6: Episode 3 & 7: Glenn and Nicholas on the Dumpster: "Thank You" & "Heads Up"
Alley on Cherry St, Hampton, GA

•S6E3 "Thank You"
Glenn and Nicholas try to escape a hoard of walkers when Nicholas leads

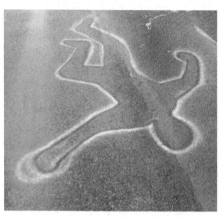

them into an alley. They retreat to a garbage dumpster where they are surrounded. Nicholas has an episode and decides to take his own life pulling Glenn off into the hoard of walkers.

•S6E7 "Heads Up"

Glenn surprisingly survives the hoard of walkers that are eating Nicholas by scooting his way under the dumpster where he remains until he is able to exit.

9. Season 6: Episode 7: Glenn Finds Enid: "Heads Up"
Cherry St, Hampton, GA

Glenn spots Enid after she throws water at him from higher up in a building. He chases after her and makes her go back to Alexandria with him.

10. Season 6: Episode 16: Road Block: "Last Day On Earth"
Old Griffin Rd, Hampton, GA

The Saviors throw a man to hang over the bridge as Rick and his group tries to get Maggie to Hilltop for care.

References

AMC. (2014). AMC. Retrieved July 15, 2014, from AMC: http://www.amctv.com/

E, C. (2011, October 9). The Walking Dead Video Locations. Retrieved August 2014, from Four Square: https://foursquare.com/ratpack/list/the-walking-dead-filming-locations

Google. (2014). Google Maps. Retrieved September 08, 2014, from Google Maps: https://maps.google.com/

The Walking Dead - Season One (2010-2014). [Television Show].

The Walking Dead - Season Two (2010-2014). [Television Show].

The Walking Dead - Season Three (2010-2014). [Television Show].

The Walking Dead - Season Four (2010-2014). [Television Show].

Wikipedia. (2014). Wikipedia. Retrieved August 23, 2014, from List of The Walking Dead episodes: http://en.wikipedia.org/wiki/List_of_The_Walking_Dead_episodes

Zee Maps. (2005-2014). Zee Maps. Retrieved September 08, 2014, from Zee Maps: https://www.zeemaps.com/

Thank you for purchasing Locations-Locations of TWD Seasons 1-6. If you would like to stay up-to-date with all the newest locations and books. Please give The Location Press a like on facebook.

The
Location
Press

Please respect owners wishes: DO NOT TRESPASS ON ANY PROPERTY!!!

CPSIA information can be obtained
at www.ICGtesting.com
Printed in the USA
FSOW03n0636230816
23970FS